FIRST
BIOGRAPHIES

Annie Oakley

Published by Raintree Steck-Vaughn Publishers, an imprint of Steck-Vaughn Company

Retold for young readers by Edith Vann
Editor: Pam Wells
Project Manager: Julie Klaus
Electronic Production: Scott Melcer

Library of Congress Cataloging-in-Publication Data

Gleiter, Jan, 1947-
    Annie Oakley / Jan Gleiter and Kathleen Thompson; illustrated by Yoshi Miyake.
       p.   cm. — (First biographies)
    ISBN 0-8114-8451-3
    1. Oakley, Annie, 1860-1926 — Juvenile literature.   2. Shooters of firearms — United States — Biography — Juvenile literature.
3. Entertainers — United States — Biography — Juvenile literature.
[1. Oakley, Annie, 1860-1926.   2. Sharpshooters.   3. Entertainers.]
I. Thompson, Kathleen.   II. Miyake, Yoshi, ill.   III. Title.   IV. Series.
GV1157.03G52   1995
799.3'092 — dc20   94-24007
[B]   CIP   AC

Printed and bound in the United States
1 2 3 4 5 6 7 8 9 0 W 99 98 97 96 95 94

FIRST BIOGRAPHIES

Annie Oakley

Jan Gleiter and Kathleen Thompson
Illustrated by Yoshi Miyake

RSVP
RAINTREE
STECK-VAUGHN
PUBLISHERS
The Steck-Vaughn Company

Austin, Texas

"I want four quail, Mr. Katzenberger," said the woman. She looked around the store. "They are for a dinner party. So I want good, fresh ones. I don't want them full of buckshot so the people break their teeth. Do you have them?"

"No," Mr. Katzenberger said. "But I will have them soon."

"How do you know they will be good?" asked the woman.

"Because that's the only kind I ever get in."

"How do you know they aren't full of buckshot?" she asked.

"Because this person uses a rifle, not a shotgun." He was trying to be patient. "This one is the best shot in Greenville. Maybe in all of Ohio," said Mr. Katzenberger.

"Then I'll wait," she said. "I hope he gets here soon."

6

Soon a tiny fourteen-year-old girl came in. She brought several quail and some furs. She had brown eyes and long brown hair. The store owner turned to the woman. "I'd like you to meet Annie Mozee."

Annie was the best shot in Greenville. She didn't know why. She just knew how to shoot from the first time she tried. So she was able to give her family meat. What they didn't need, she sold in town. She gave them the money to buy their farm.

With Annie's help, things began to get better. Life had been very hard for Annie's family. They had been very poor. Now Mr. Katzenberger bought as many quail as she could bring in. He also bought beaver and mink furs from her.

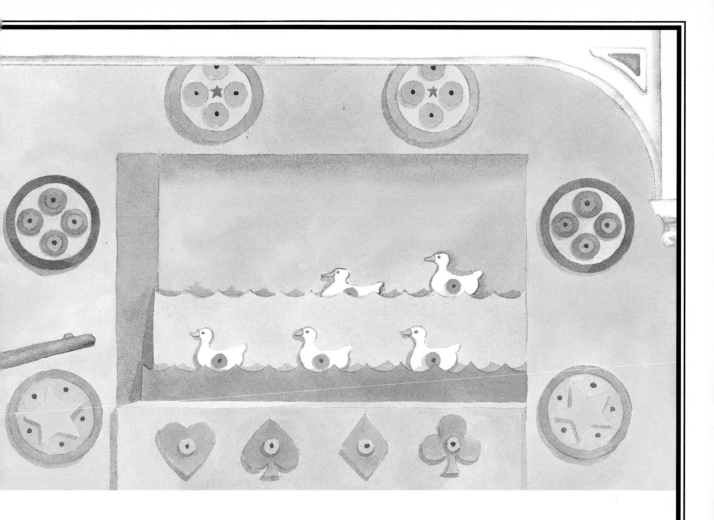

In 1875 Annie was fifteen. She went to live in Cincinnati, Ohio, with her older sister. Once she went to a place to practice shooting. Her sister's husband liked to shoot at the moving metal ducks.

He said to Annie, "I hear you've done some shooting. Why don't you try?"

Annie shot six times. Six ducks fell over. The owner was surprised. He told her to try again. Again six ducks fell over.

The owner of the gallery set up a contest. It was between Annie and Frank Butler. Butler was a trick shooter. When he saw Annie, Butler was surprised. Her rifle was about as tall as she was. Some people laughed at Annie. But when she started shooting, nobody laughed.

Each would shoot at twenty-five clay plates called "pigeons." They took turns. Time after time neither one missed. On Butler's last shot, he missed. Annie won the contest with her last shot!

Frank Butler was not angry that he had lost. He asked Annie to come to his trick-shooting show. She wanted to see what he could do. There was something about this smiling man that she liked.

Annie saw Frank's show. Then she saw it again. Before long they were married.

"I lost a shooting contest," said Frank with a smile. "But I won a wife."

Soon Frank and Annie started their own show. "A show called **Butler and Butler** doesn't sound right. We need a new name for you," Frank said.

"I've always liked Oakley," said Annie. So Butler and Oakley did shows all over.

Annie had a lot to learn. She knew all about shooting. Frank knew how to put on a lively, fast-moving show.

"At first, people like to see you just stand and

shoot. But not for long. You'll have to make it more exciting," he said.

So soon Annie shot at things while she rode around the ring on a horse. She shot cards out of Frank's hand. She hit glass balls tossed in the air.

It wasn't easy to keep a show going. So Annie and Frank went to work for the Sells Brothers Circus. Going from place to place was hard. Then the circus's money started running out.

Annie and Frank wanted to leave the circus. Soon they heard about Buffalo Bill's Wild West Show.

People who lived in the East loved shows about the West. Buffalo Bill's show was liked the most. Buffalo Bill had hunted buffalo. He had also been a great scout for the army. His show had American Indians, cowboys, and horses. There were deer, bears, and, of course, buffalo.

Annie and Frank wanted to work for the Wild West Show.

Buffalo Bill was not sure. He said, "I want somebody who can shoot from the back of a horse. I want somebody who can shoot an apple off a dog's head."

The somebody was Annie Oakley.

Annie and Frank joined the show in 1885. Annie was called "The Little Girl of the Western Plains." She had never been west of the Mississippi River. But she gave the people a great show.

In one trick she turned her back to Frank. She held her rifle backward. Frank would spin a glass ball on a string. She took aim by looking into a mirror. She always hit the ball the first time.

Another trick was to miss an easy shot. Then several things would fly into the air at once. Annie would hit every one.

Buffalo Bill knew people would like to see the Sioux leader, Sitting Bull. In 1876 General Custer had lost to the Sioux at the Battle of the Little Bighorn. Sitting Bull said he would stay with the show for one year. Times were hard. His people needed the money he could make in the show.

Sitting Bull did not like being in the show. But he loved to watch Annie's act. "Little Sure Shot!" he called her.

He liked Annie very much. Sitting Bull adopted her as his daughter.

Sitting Bull and Annie Oakley were earning money in the Wild West Show. They remembered when they never had enough money. They also thought of the people they had left behind. Sitting Bull sent money to his family. He gave money to other people who needed it, too.

Sitting Bull told Annie about his children back home. He had eleven of his own. He had also taken in homeless children. He was lonely for his family.

Annie remembered being lonely for her family, too. As a child, she had spent many years away from them. Those years had been sad and hard.

Annie's family had been very poor. Her father and later her stepfather died. Her mother had a hard time feeding all her children.

When Annie was nine, she left home. She got a job in a home for poor people. She earned only her food and clothes. But that helped her family.

When Annie was eleven, she heard about another job. Annie wanted that job, working for a farmer. She could get fifty cents a week.

"I want a girl who will cook and carry water," said the farmer.

"I'll cook and carry," said Annie.

"I wanted a bigger girl," said the farmer's wife.

"I'll grow," said Annie.

At the farm Annie milked the cows and fed the pigs. She washed the floors and took care of the baby. She cooked and washed dishes. She couldn't go to school. She never got the fifty cents a week. So Annie ran away.

Annie found her way home. Her mother kissed her and cried. Annie was happy to be with the people who loved her. One day she fired a rifle. She had found something she could do better than anyone else in the world.

Annie never forgot what it was like to be a child. The Wild West Show went to New York. There Annie visited a home for children without mothers and fathers. She asked them to come to the show. Fifty children came and liked it very much. The show sent free tickets to other New York homes for children. Then the show had a special "Annie Oakley Day."

The Wild West Show went all over the world. It went to England, France, Spain, and Italy. Then it went to Greenville, Ohio, the town Annie came from.

Welcome Home Annie Oakley

Twenty thousand people came. Her mother and her sisters came. Everyone wanted to see her shoot a coin from her husband's fingers. She had shot straight for twenty-five years. Everyone wanted to see the best shot in the world. And everyone did.

Key Dates

1860   Annie Oakley is born in Darke County, Ohio, on August 13. Her name is Phoebe Anne Oakley Mozee.

1868   Learns to shoot at the age of eight.

1875   Wins a shooting contest with Frank Butler.

1876   Marries Frank Butler. Takes the stage name of Annie Oakley.

1885   Stars in Buffalo Bill's Wild West Show. Annie once hit 943 out of 1,000 glass balls thrown in the air.

1901   Retires from the Wild West Show, after being hurt in a train accident. Annie keeps on performing for twenty years.

1914–1918   Gives shows and teaches American soldiers how to shoot during World War I.

1926   Annie Oakley dies in Greenville, Ohio, on November 3.

WITHDRAWN